Walter Jacobs

Jacobs' Easy Banjo Mandolin and Banjo Orchestra Folio

1st & 2nd Banjos

Walter Jacobs

Jacobs' Easy Banjo Mandolin and Banjo Orchestra Folio
1st & 2nd Banjos

ISBN/EAN: 9783337393625

Printed in Europe, USA, Canada, Australia, Japan

Cover: Foto ©Thomas Meinert / pixelio.de

More available books at **www.hansebooks.com**

Jacobs' Easy

No. I.

1st & 2nd BANJOS

MANDOLIN & BANJO ORCHESTRA FOLIO

Prices and Combinations.

Solo Mandolin	.	.50
Mandolin and Guitar	.	1.00
2 Mandolins and Guitar	.	1 50
2 Mands., Mandola and Guitar		2 00
3 Mandolins and Guitar	.	2.00
Mandolin and Piano	.	1.00
2 Mandolins and Piano	.	1.50
2 Mands., Mandola and Piano		2.00
3 Mandolins and Piano	.	2.00
Mandolin, Guitar and Piano		1.50
2 Mandolins, Guitar and Piano		2.00
2 M's, M'dola or 3d M., G. and P.		2.50
Mandolin and 1 or 2 Banjos		1.00
1 or 2 Banjos	.	.50
" " and Guitar	.	1.00
" " and Piano		1.00
" " Guitar and Piano		1.50
" " Mandolin and G'tar		1.50
" " 2 M's and Guitar		2.00
" " Man., G. and Piano		2.00
" " 2 M's, G. and P.		2.50
" " 2 M's, Mandola or		
3d M., Guitar and Piano		3.00
Flute part (Obligato)	.	.50
'Cello part (Obligato)	.	.50
Violin and Piano	.	1.00

INSTRUMENTATION.

1st 2nd 3rd MANDOLINS
(AND MANDOLA)
FLUTE
'CELLO
1st & 2nd BANJOS
GUITAR &
PIANO
ACCOMPANIMENTS

17 ORIGINAL COMPOSITIONS AND ARRANGEMENTS BY VARIOUS POPULAR COMPOSERS

~PUBLISHED BY~

WALTER JACOBS,
BOSTON, MASS.
COPYRIGHT, 1899 BY WALTER JACOBS

EACH BOOK COMPLETE .50

CONTENTS.

(SEE NOTE.)

NOTE: As all the pieces in this Folio are published in sheet music form also, single extra parts for any of the eight instruments can be obtained. The 1st and 2nd Banjo parts are printed together on the same sheet and therefore cannot be had seperately.

Jacobs' Easy Mandolin and Banjo Orchestra Folio. 200-196

PRINCE CHARMING.
Waltz.

By H. P. DUFFELL.
Arr. by WALTER JACOBS.

NOTE: A figure encircled thus, ③ signifies the string.

1×3-3

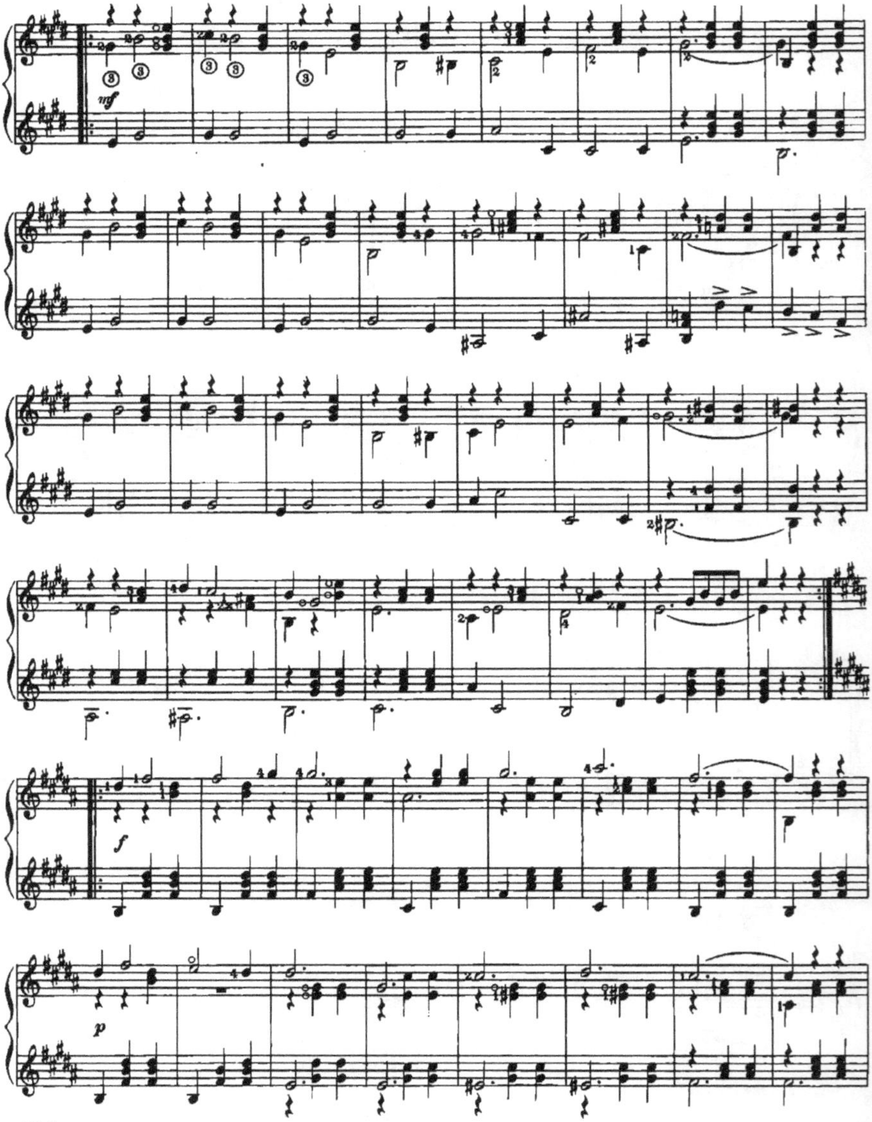
mf
f
p

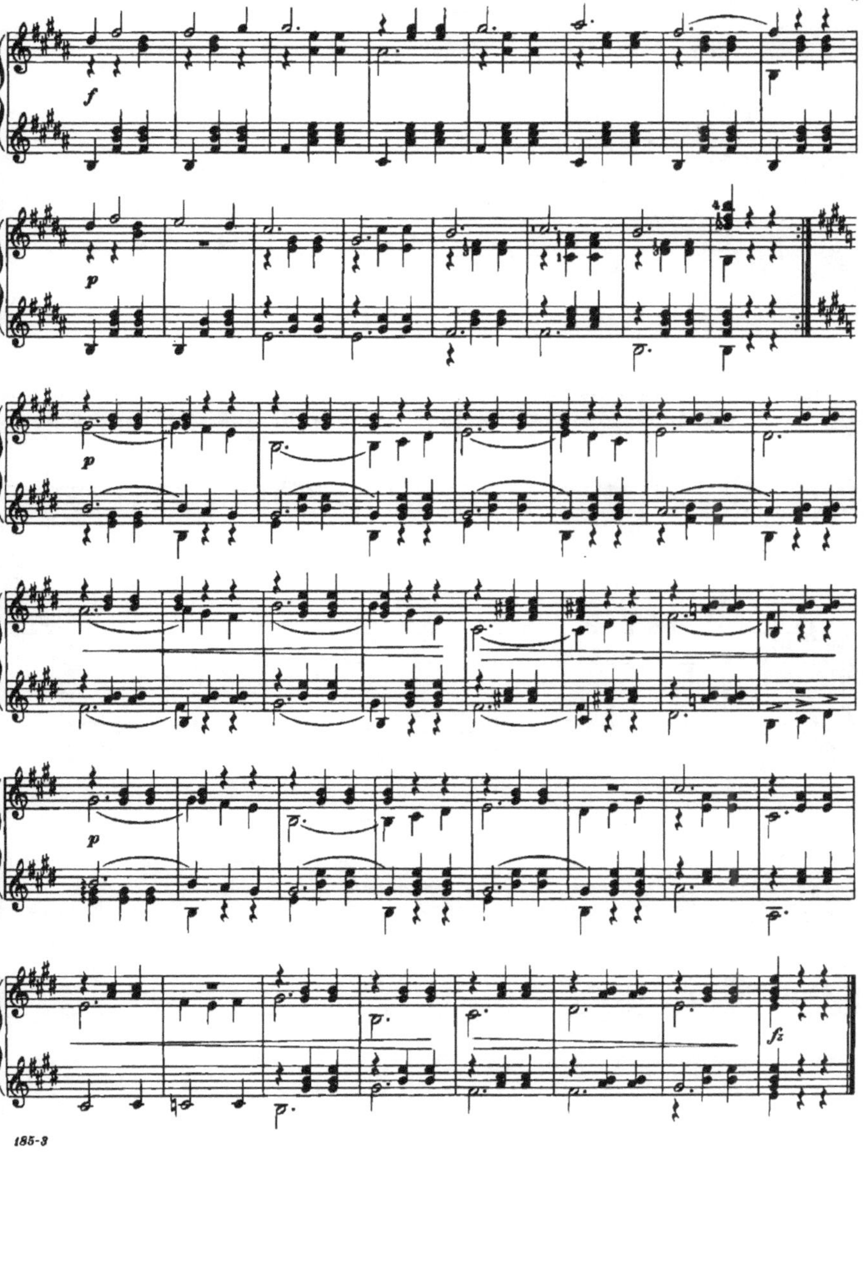
f
p
p
p
fz

MONTCLAIR GALOP.

A. J. WEIDT.

NOTE: A figure encircled thus, ④ signifies the string.

188-3

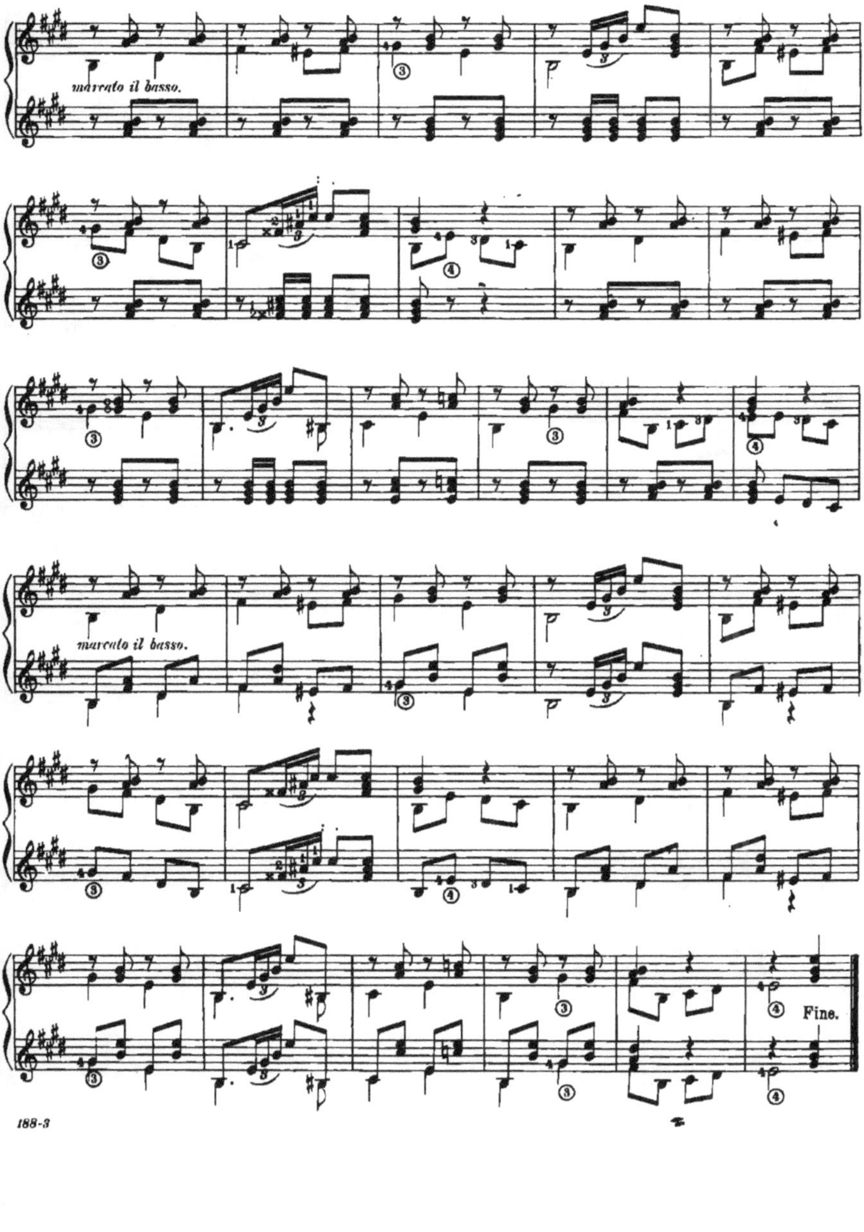
marcato il basso.
marcato il basso.
Fine.

TRIO.

D.C. al Fine.

MYRA WALTZ.

Piano acc. 25cts.
Guitar acc. 15cts.

By GEO. W. BEMIS.

SOLO BANJO.

2nd BANJO.

WALTZ.

177-3

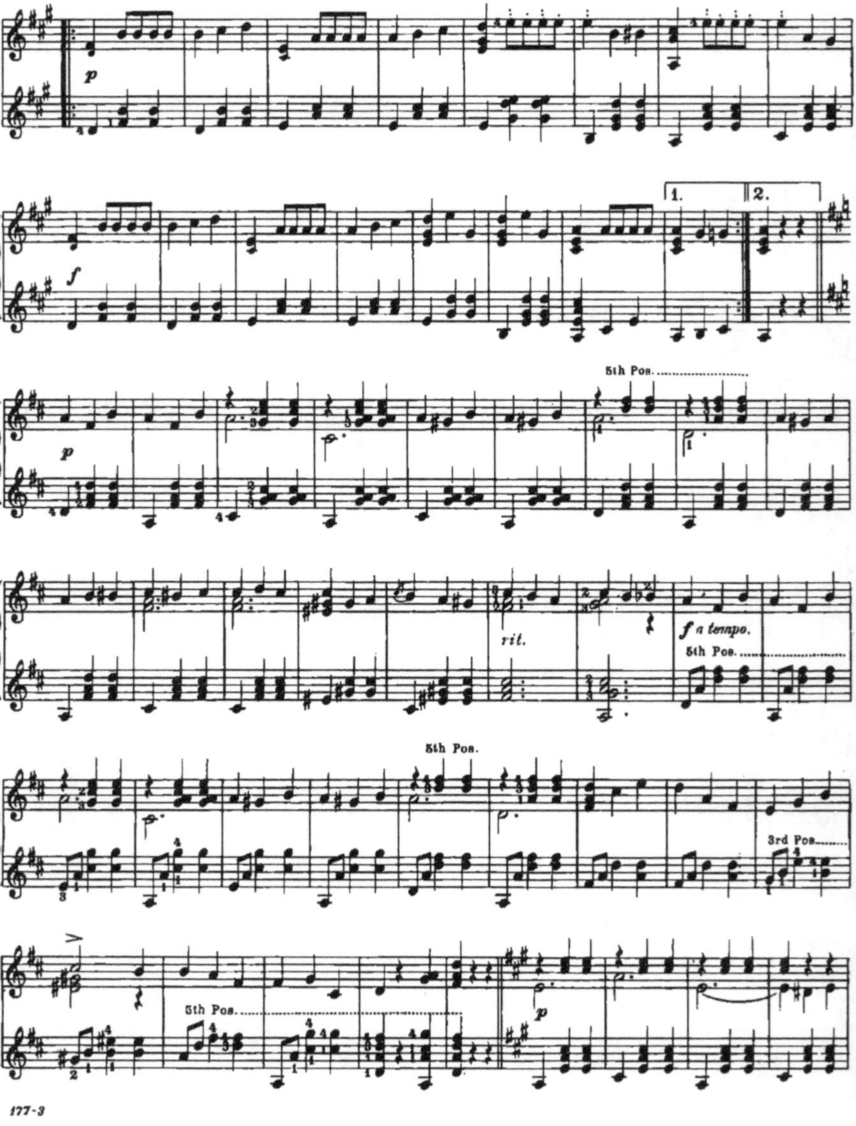
p
f
1.
2.
5th Pos.
p
rit.
f a tempo.
5th Pos.
5th Pos.
3rd Pos.
5th Pos.
p

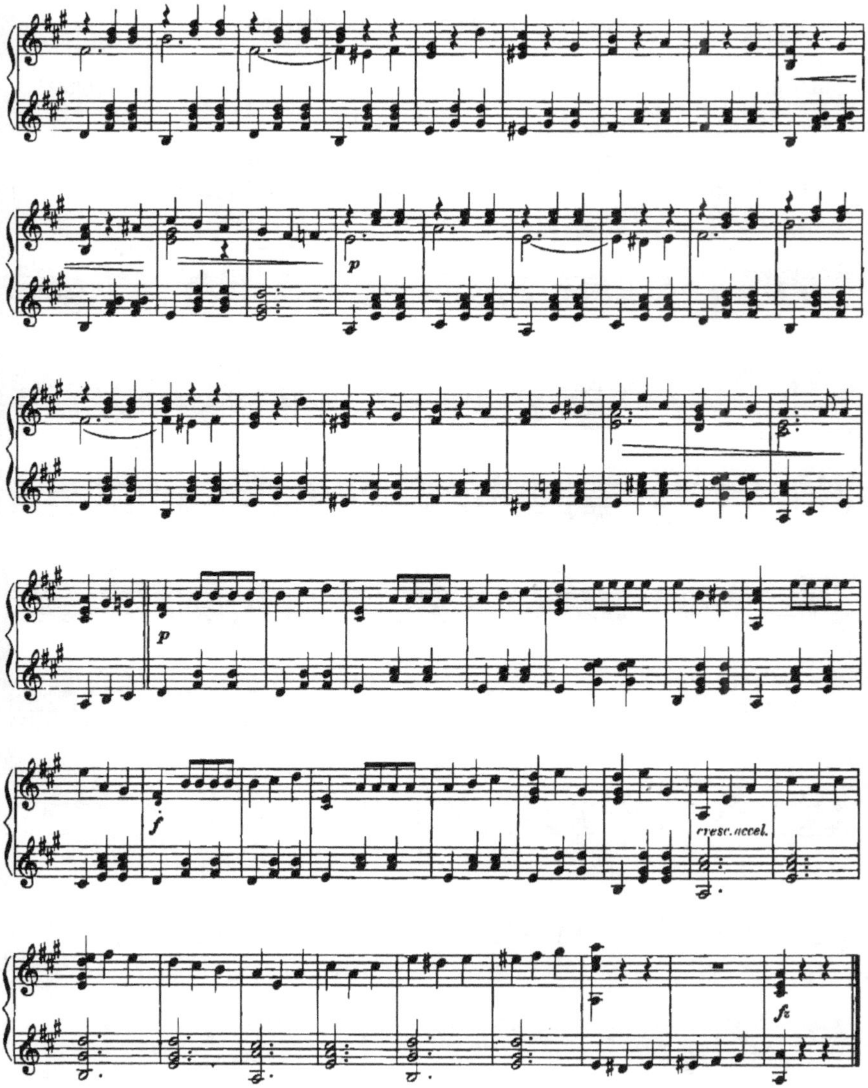
p
p
f
cresc. accel.
fz

1 or 2 Banjos... 30 cts.
1 or 2 Mandolins 30 cts.
1 or 2 Guitars...30 cts.
Guitar acc.10 cts.
Piano acc.10 cts.

"NEW HARP" SCHOTTISCHE.

FOR ONE OR TWO BANJOS AND GUITAR.

SOLO BANJO.

By R. S. SAUNDERS.

Tempo di Schottische.

GUITAR Acc.
1 or 2 Guitars.30

By R. S. SAUNDERS.

Tempo di Schottische.

TRIO.

D.C. al Fine.

1 or 2 Banjos.30
BANJO Acc.

Arr. by JACOBS.

"NEW HARP" SCHOTTISCHE.

Tempo di Schottische.

TRIO.

D.C. al Fine.

61-3

To E. A. Jr. and Gerald D. Boardman, Boston.

DARKIE'S HOEDOWN.

One or two Banjos, with Guitar and Piano Acc.

1 or 2 Mandolins 20cts.
1 or 2 Guitars . . . 30cts.

By WALTER JACOBS Op.107.

Lively.

Solo Banjo.

Guitar Teachers. Try "Little Sinners Waltz." for one or two Guitars. Price 30¢

21 - 3

DARKIE'S HOEDOWN.

One or two Banjos, with Guitar and Piano Acc.

WALTER JACOBS. Op.107.

DARKIE'S HOEDOWN.

21 - 3

March.

FOR 1 OR 2 BANJOS.

By J. F. WAGNER.
Arr. by WALTER JACOBS.

BASS SOLO ON 4th STRING.

ON BASS STRING.

Fine.

TRIO.

IN HIGH SOCIETY.

MARCH AND TWO-STEP.

FOR 1 OR 2 BANJOS WITH PIANO AND GUITAR ACC.

By EDUARD HOLST.
Arr. by WALTER JACOBS.

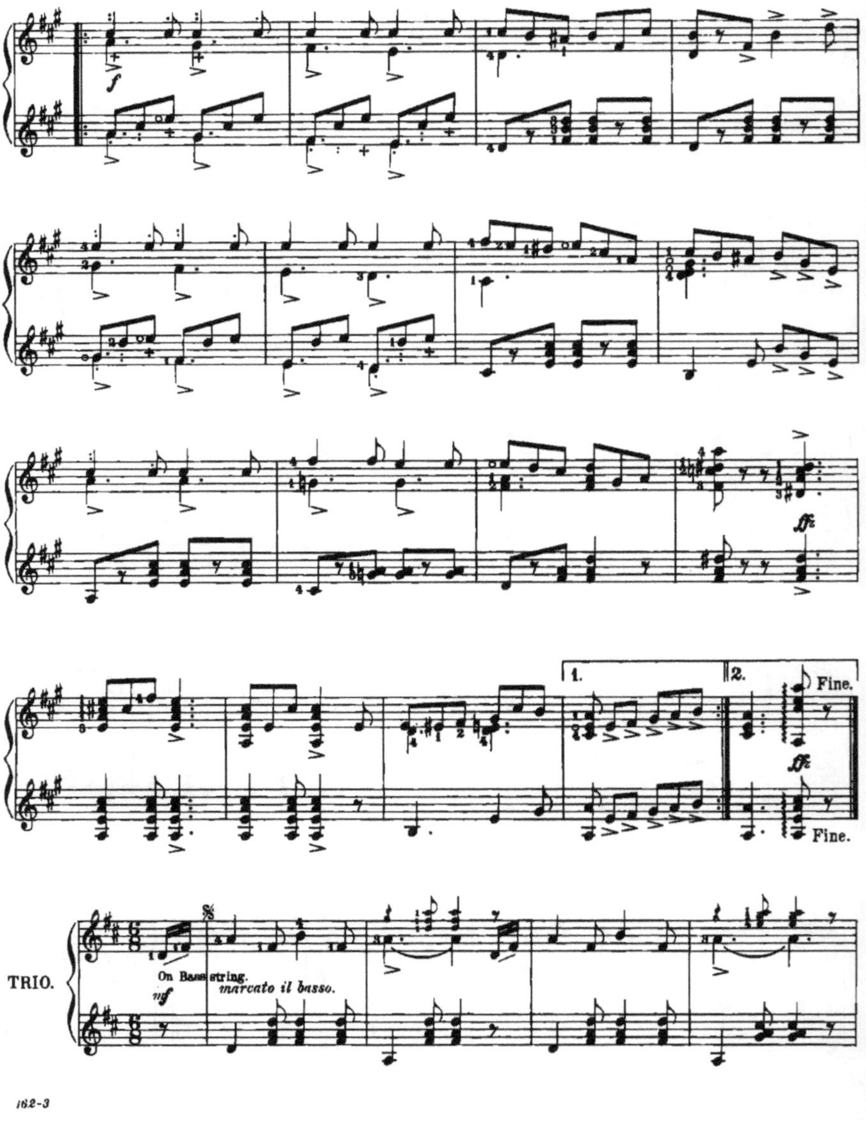
f
ffz
1.
2.
Fine.
ffz
Fine.
TRIO.
On Bass string.
mf
marcato il basso.

8va ad lib.
10 Pos
7 Pos
1st time only.
Last time only.
D.C. al Fine.
D. S. Trio al

To my niece Corinne C. Dooley.

LITTLE SUNBEAM WALTZ.

1 or 2 Guitars 30 cts.

For one or two Banjos and Guitar,
with 1st and 2d Mandolin parts.

By C. S. De LANO.

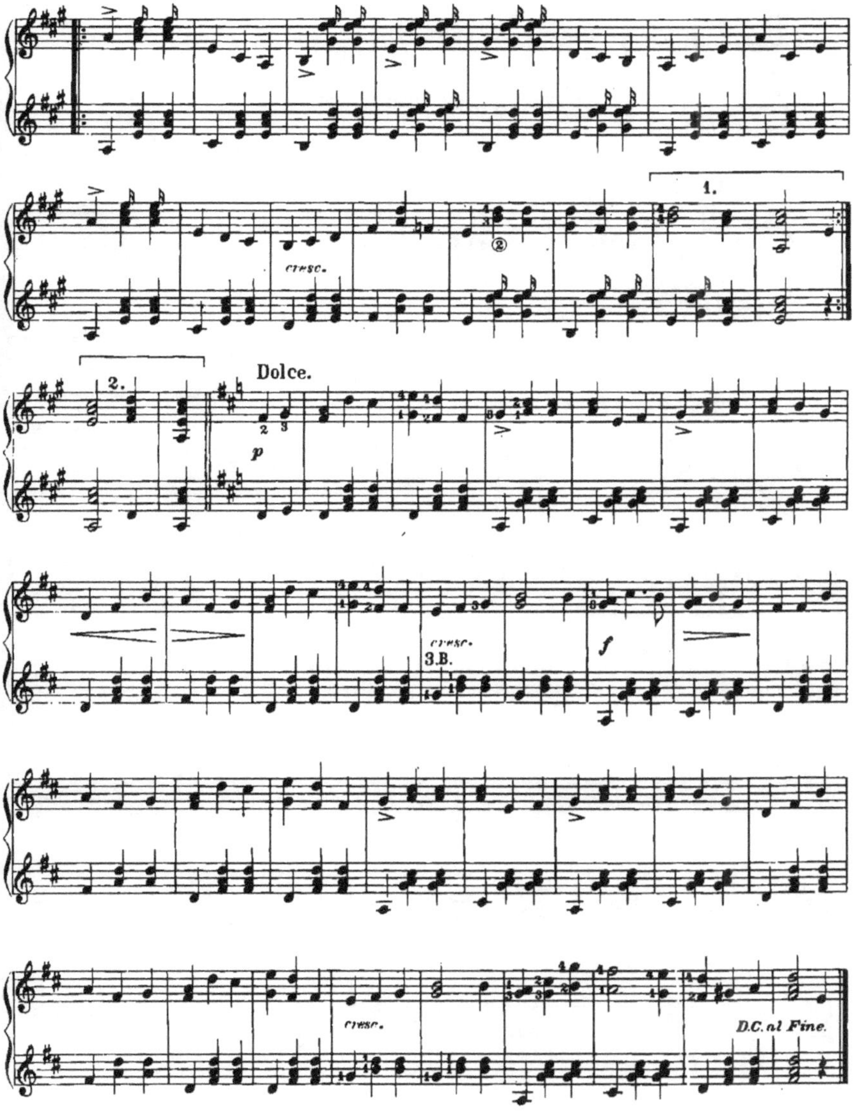
1.
cresc.
2.
Dolce.
p
cresc.
3.B.
f
cresc.
D.C. al Fine.

To Miss Sarah Osgood, Boston.

1 or 2 Mandolins......30 cts.
1 or 2 Banjos...........40 cts.
Guitar Solo.............30 cts.
Guitar acc.....10 cts.
Piano acc.......25 cts.
Banjo acc......10 cts.

"HOWDY" DARKIES!

FOR ONE OR TWO BANJOS.

By WALTER JACOBS, Op. 145.

BASS ELEVATED.

Andante. *con espressione.*

BANJO.

Copyright 1896 by Walter Jacobs.

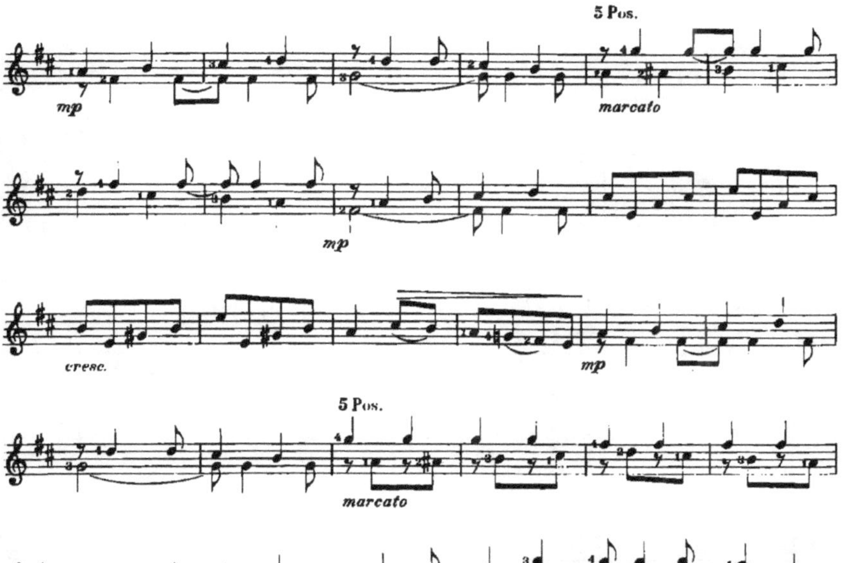
5 Pos.
mp
marcato
mp
cresc.
mp
5 Pos.
marcato
mp
cresc.
mf
f

OVER THE WAVES.

(SOBRE LAS OLAS.)

Waltzes.

JUVENTINO ROSAS.
Arr. by WALTER JACOBS.

Fine.
ff energico.
sentimental.
ff energico.
p
1.
2.
D.C.
No.1. al Fine
a poi No.2.

2.
tremolo sempre.
On 3rd String.
mf
tremolo sempre.
On 4th String.
1st String.
2nd String.
3rd String.
1st String.
2nd.
4th.
1.
2.
ff
pp
p

CODA.

D.C. No. 1. al 🔴 a poi Coda.

cresc. - poco - poco - rall. - rit. f a tempo, tremolo.

3rd String.

4th String.

tremolo.

ff

tremolo.

SONG AND DANCE SCHOTTISCHE.

By W. D. KENNETH.

Copyright 1894 by W. D. Kenneth.

DANCE. Allegro.

1 or 2 Guitars 30cts.
Piano Acc. . . .40cts.

FLOWER WALTZ.

For one or two Banjos.

By WALTER JACOBS. Op. 39.

SOLO BANJO.
Tune Bass to B.

2nd BANJO.

Guitar, Mandolin, Banjo.
W. J.

Copyright 1894, by Walter Jacobs.

3 - 2

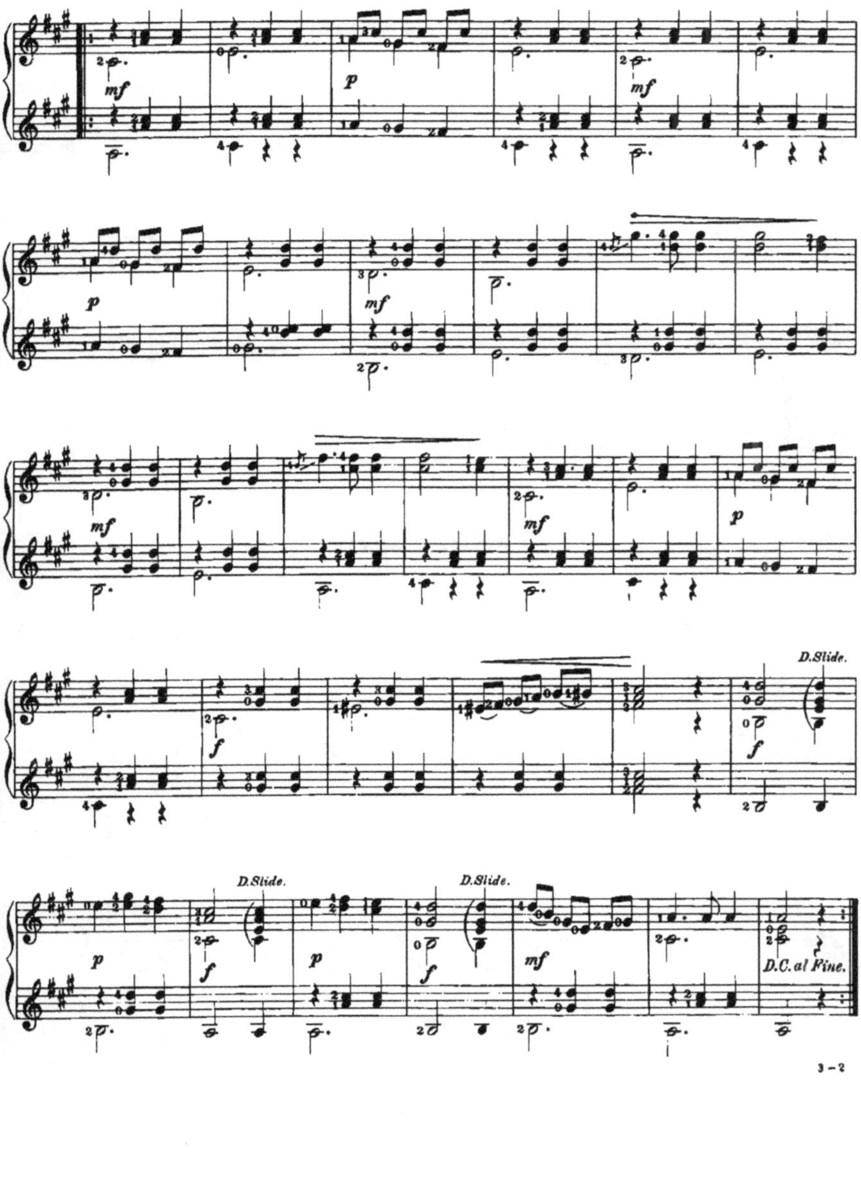
D.Slide.
D.Slide.
D.Slide.
D.C. al Fine.

THE GOLDEN DOME.

MARCH AND TWO-STEP.

By WALTER JACOBS.

Copyright 1898 by Walter Jacobs. Boston.

9 Pos.

Solo Banjo can play either first or second staff.

cresc.

f on repeat.

D. S. al 𝄐 then Trio.

f on repeat.

D. S. al 𝄐 then Trio.

TRIO.

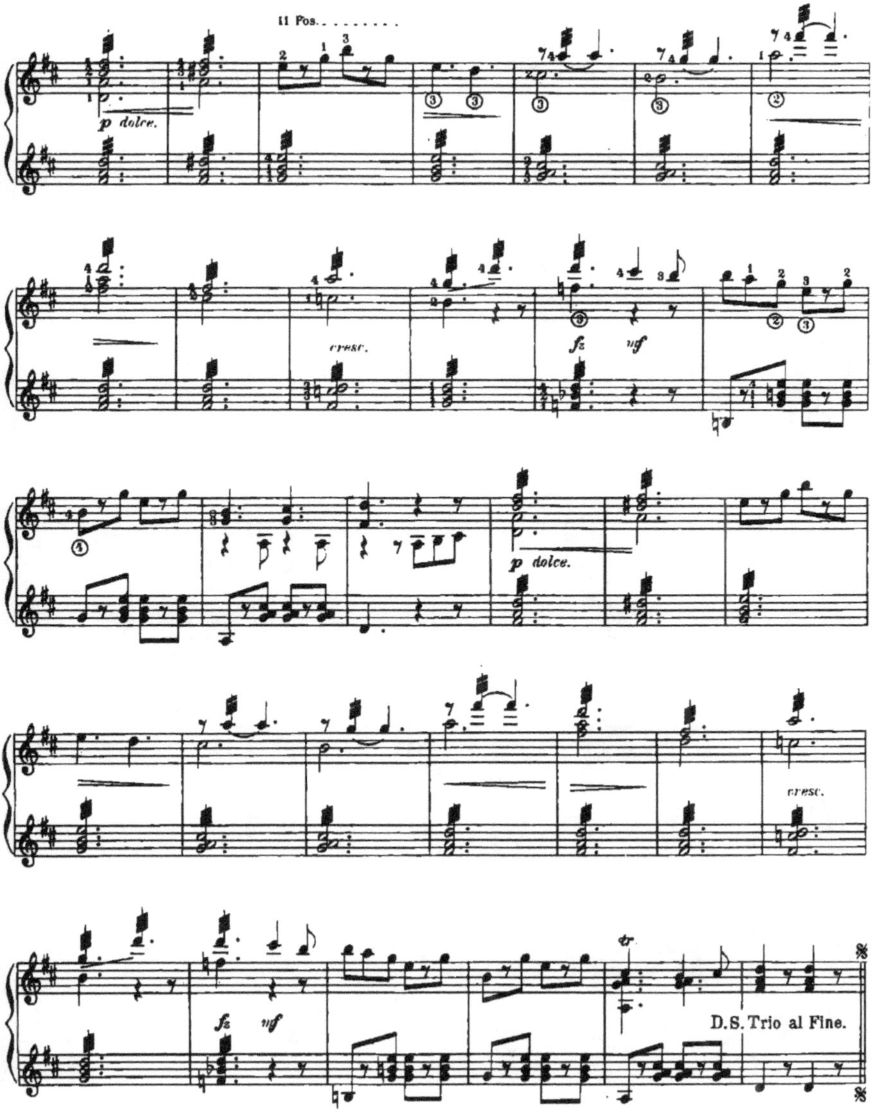
II Pos. . . . .
p dolce.
cresc.
fz
mf
p dolce.
cresc.
fz
mf
tr
D.S. Trio al Fine.

To Miss Gerta Hatch, Los Angeles.

LA VETA SCHOTTISCHE.

For one or two Banjos and Guitar
with 1st and 2d Mandolin parts.

By C. S. DeLANO.

Composer of Little Sunbeam Waltz.

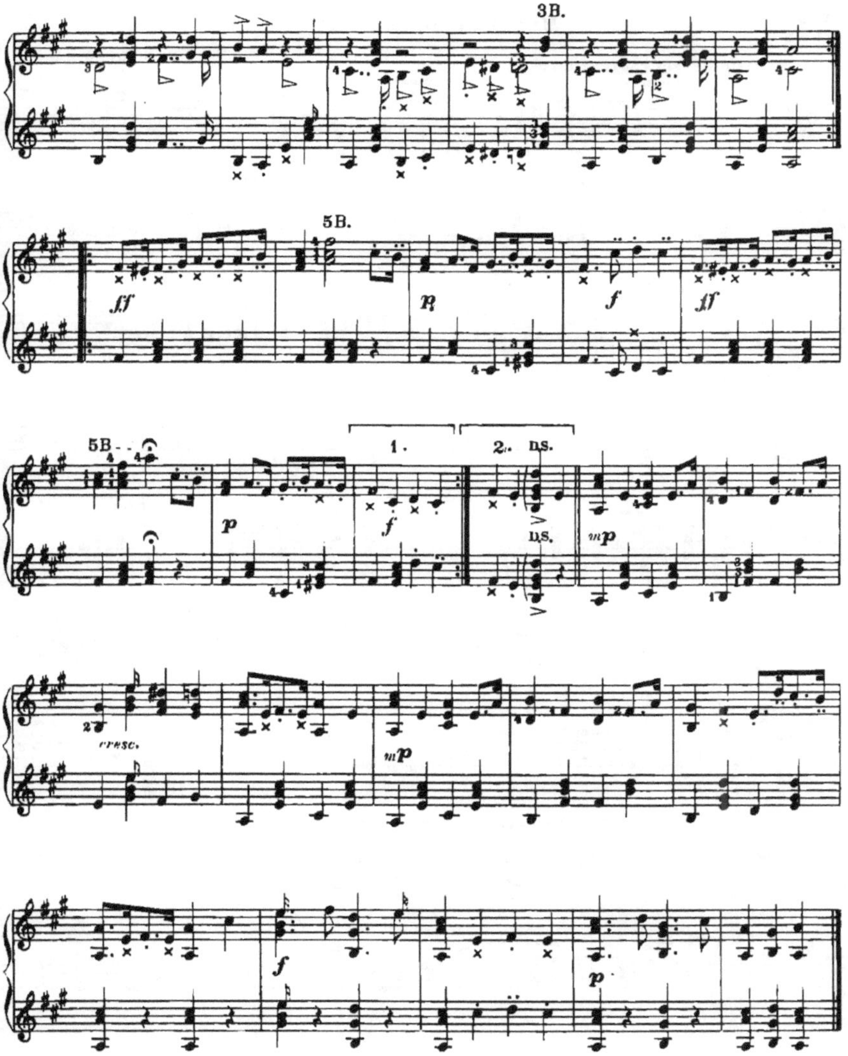
3B.
5B.
ff
p
f
ff
5B
1.
2.
DS.
mp
cresc.
mp
f
p

HEART SO TRUE.

MAZURKA DE CONCERT.

BANJO.
BASS to B.

By WALTER JACOBS.

Andante con espressione.

Tempo di Mazurka. **Animato.**

(Piano or Guitar.)

Fine.

D.S. al Fine.

195-2

5th
cresc.
cresc.
dim.
cresc.
rall.
a tempo.
rit.
poco a poco.
a tempo.
rit.
a tempo.
cresc.
Più lento.
cresc.
e
accel.
stringendo.
rit.

SPANISH DANCE.
No 1.

FOR 1 OR 2 BANJOS WITH PIANO AND GUITAR ACC.

Tune Banjo to D.

MORITZ MOSZKOWSKI, Op.12.
Arr. by WALTER JACOBS.

Allegro brioso.

SOLO BANJO.

2nd BANJO.

10 Pos.
3 Pos.
4 Pos.
6 Pos.
2 Pos.
4 Pos.
p e grazioso.
2 Pos.
4 Pos.
2 Pos.
14 Pos.
16 Pos.
marcato.
p
2 Pos.
4 Pos.

44

SCHOTTISCHE.

By A.H. PLANTE.
Arr. by WALTER JACOBS.

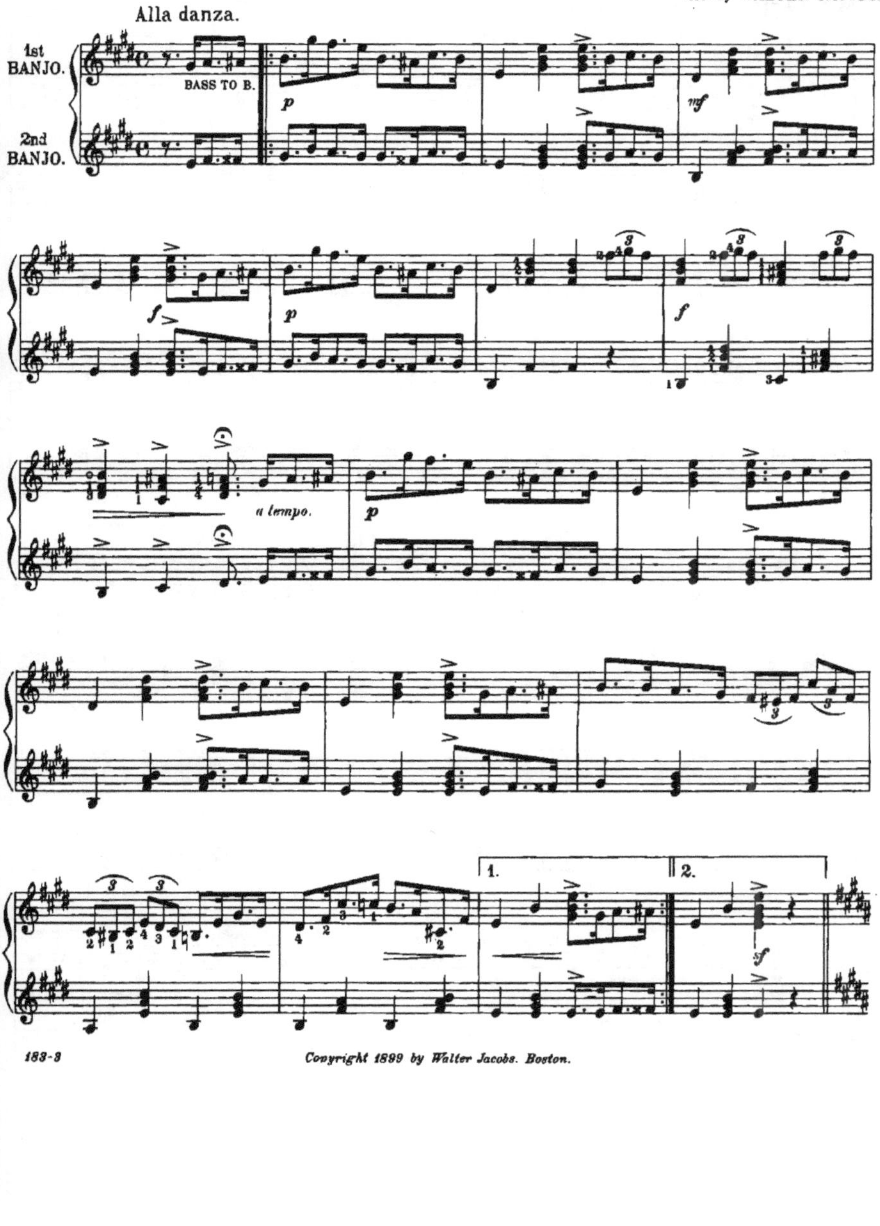

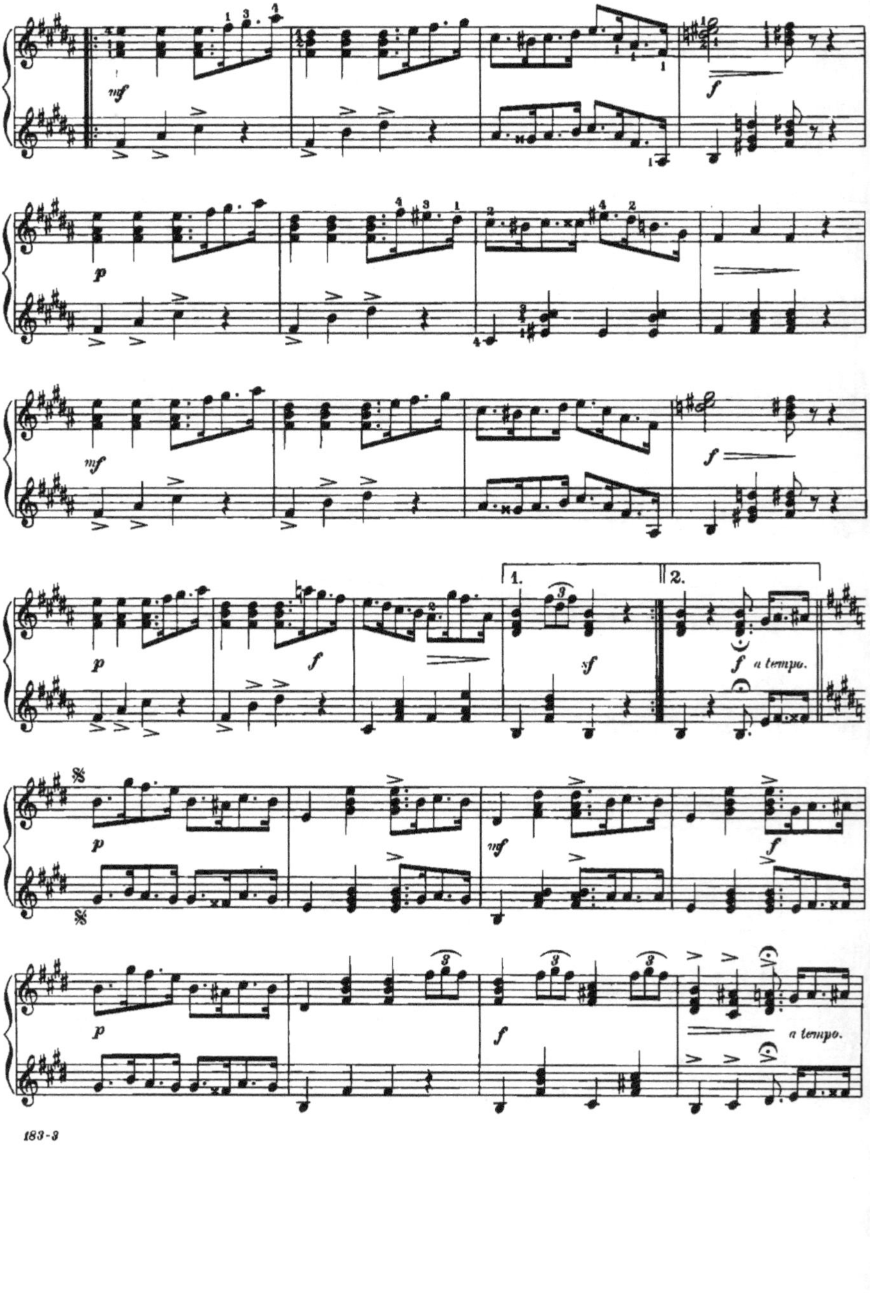
1.
2.
a tempo.
a tempo.

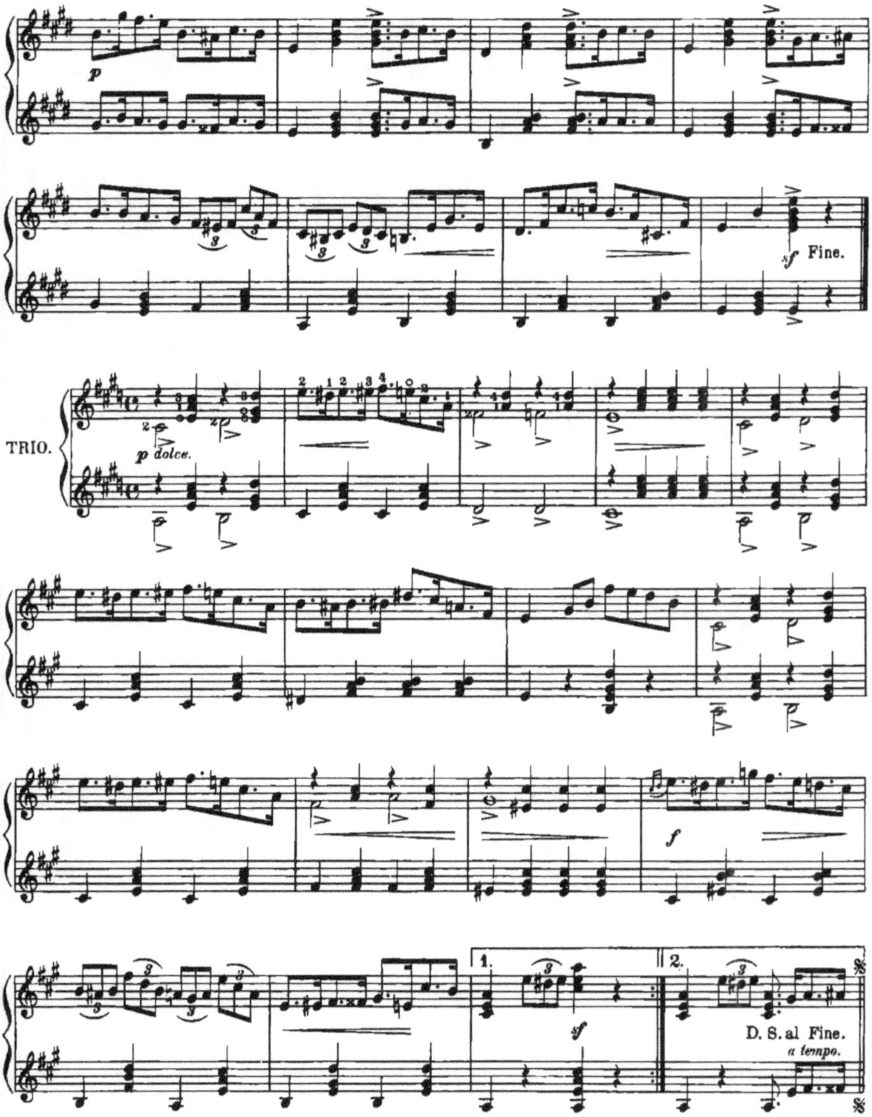
p
sf Fine.
TRIO.
p dolce.
f
sf
D. S. al Fine.
a tempo.

Banjo Music

Degrees of difficulty are marked thus:
A, Easy B, Medium C, Difficult

When the price of the Banjo Solo is the same as the Banjo Accompaniment the two parts are printed together, and therefore cannot be obtained separately.

Title	Composer / Arranger	Grade	Banjo Solo	Banjo Acc.	Guitar Acc.	Piano Acc.
'A Frangesa March. (Costa)	Arr. Jacobs	B	.40	.15	.10	.20
African Smile, An. Characteristic March	Eno	B	.40	.15	.10	.20
Ah Sin. Eccentric Two-Step Novelty. (Rolfe)	Arr. Jacobs	B	.40	.15	.10	.20
Airy Fairy. Schottische	Weidt	A	.30	.30	.10	.20
Alabama Kickiets. Cake Walk	Lansing	A	.30	.30	.10	.20
Alpine Flowers. Waltz	Weidt	A	.30	.30	.10	.20
Always Happy. Schottische	Simpson	A	.30	.15	.10	.20
Among the Flowers. Caprice	Eno	A	.40	.15	.10	.20
Anita. Spanish Serenade. (Allen)	Arr. Jacobs	B	.40	.15	.10	.20
Any Rags? Schottische. (Allen)	Arr. Jacobs-Hildreth	B	.40	.15	.10	.20
Arbitrator, The. March and Two-Step	Arr. Hildreth-Jacobs	B	.40	.15	.10	.20
Assembly, The. March and Two-Step	Eno	A	.40	.15	.10	.20
At the Club. March	Weidt	A	.40	.15	.10	.20
Barn Dance. (The Bunnies' Gambol) (Rice)	Arr. Jacobs	B	.40	.15	.10	.20
Bean Club Musings. March Characteristic	Eno	B	.40	.15	.10	.20
Beggar's Dance. Polka Two-Step	Weidt	A	.40	.15	.10	.20
Behind the Hounds. March and Two-Step	Arr. Jacobs	A	.40	.15	.10	.20
Bells of Moscow. Mazurka. (Aletter)	Arr. Jacobs	B	.40	.15	.10	.20
Big Chief Battle-Axe. (Allen) Indian Novelty Two-Step	Arr. Hildreth-Jacobs	B	.40	.15	.10	.20
Black Cupid, The. Schottische	Weidt	A	.40	.15	.10	.20
Bostonian, The. March and Two-Step	Kenneth	A	.40	.40	.10	.20
Boston Yodle, The. Dance a la Far Janeo	Weidt	A	.40	.40	.10	.20
Boys' Brigade, The. March	Lansing	A	.30	.30	.10	.20
Boys of the Militia. March. (Boehnlein)	Arr. Hildreth-Jacobs	B	.40	.15	.10	.20
Bucking Broncho, The. Intermezzo Two-Step	Arr. Hildreth	B	.40	.15	.10	.20
Budding Rose, The. Mazurka	Weidt	A	.40	.15	.10	.20
By the Watermelon Vine. (Lindy Lou) Schottische	Arr. Jacobs	B	.40	.15	.10	.20
Chicken Pickin's. Dance Descriptive. (Allen)	Arr. Jacobs	B	.40	.15	.10	.20
Chirpers, The. Morceau Characteristic	Frank	B	.40	.15	.10	.20
Colored Guards, The. Characteristic March	Weidt	A	.30	.30	.10	.20
Country Dance, A. (Brown)	Arr. Jacobs	B	.40	.15	.10	.20
Cupid's Glance. Waltzes	Eno	B	.50	.25	.20	.35
Cupids on Parade. March and Two-Step	Lansing	A	.40	.15	.10	.20
Cupid's Victory. Waltz	Weidt	A	.30	.30	.10	.20
Dance of the Phantoms	Farrand	B	.40	..	..	.20
Dance of the Skeletons. Descriptive. (Allen)	Arr. Jacobs	B	.40	.15	.10	.20
Dancing Goddess, The. Caprice. (Hildreth)	Arr. Weidt	B	.40	.15	.10	.20
Darkies' Drill, The. Two-Step Cake Walk	Jacobs-Hildreth	B	.40	.15	.10	.20
Darkies' Holiday, The. Sidewalk Shuffle	Arr. Hildreth	A	.40	.15	.10	.20
Darkville Favorite, The. A Dance	Kenneth	A	.30	.15	..	..
Dickey Dance, The. Caprice Humoresque	Lansing	B	.40	.15	.10	.20
Dinah's Soiree. Cake Walk	Lansing	A	.40	.15	.10	.20
Dixie Antics. A Darkey Exhilaration	Lansing	B	.40	..	..	..
Dixie Rube, The. Characteristic March. (Allen)	Arr. Jacobs	B	.40	.15	.10	.20
Dixie Twilight. Characteristic March. (Johnson)	Arr. Jacobs	B	.40	..	..	..
Down the Pike. March and Two-Step	Weidt	B	.40	.15	.10	.20
Drowsy Dempsey. A Coon Shuffle	Lansing	B	.40	.15	.10	.20
Dushka. Russian Dance	Lansing	A	.30	.30	.10	.20
Elephant Promenade. A Toe Tickler. (Saunders)	Arr. Jacobs	B	.40	.15	.10	.20
Fairy Flirtations. Dance Caprice. (Boehnlein)	Arr. Jacobs	B	.40	.15	.10	.20
Fanchette. Tambourine Dance. (Hildreth)	Arr. Jacobs	B	.40	.15	.10	.20
Fanchon. Mazurka	Weidt	A	.30	.30	.10	.20
Farmer Bungtown. March Humoresque	Arr. Hildreth-Jacobs	B	.40	.15	.10	.20
Fire-fly. Polka	Weidt	A	.30	.30	.10	.20
Flower Waltz	Jacobs	A	.40	.40	.10	.20
For the Flag. Military March Two-Step	Hildreth-Jacobs	B	.40	.15	.10	.20
Four Little Blackberries. Schottische. (O'Connor)	Arr. Jacobs	B	.40	.15	.10	.20
Frost King, The. March and Two-Step	Kenneth	A	.40	.15	.10	.20
Fun in a Barber Shop. Novelty March. (Winne)	Arr. Jacobs	B	.40	.15	.10	.20
General Jasper Jones. Cake Walk Two-Step	Lansing	B	.30	..	..	..
Good-bye Mister Greenback. Schottische	Arr. Jacobs-Hildreth	B	.40	.15	.10	.20
Guest of Honor, The. March and Two-Step	Arr. Jacobs	B	.40	.15	.10	.20
Happy Hayseed, The. Characteristic March	Arr. Hildreth	B	.40	.15	.10	.20
Happy Jap, The. Geisha Dance. (O'Connor)	Arr. Jacobs	B	.40	.15	.10	.20
Haters, The. March and Two-Step	Weidt	A	.40	.15	.10	.20
Heart Murmurs. Waltz. (Rolfe)	Arr. Hildreth	B	.40	.25	.20	.35
Hey! Mister Joshua. Medley Schottische	Arr. Jacobs	B	.40	.15	.10	.20
Home, Sweet Home and Spanish Fandango	Arr. Jacobs	A	.30	..	..	..
Hoop-e-Kack. Two-Step Novelty (Allen)	Arr. Hildreth-Jacobs	B	.40	.15	.10	.20
Horse Marines, The. March and Two-Step. (Allen)	Jacobs	B	.40	.15	.10	.20
Idabel. Waltz	Weidt	A	.30	.30	.10	.20
Idolizers, The. March and Two-Step. (Corey)	Arr. Weidt	B	.40	.15	.10	.20
In a Rose Garden. Polka Redowa. (Allen)	Arr. Weidt	B	.40	.15	.10	.20
Jack in the Box. Character Dance. (Allen)	Arr. Jacobs	B	.40	.15	.10	.20
Jasper's Symphony	Lansing	B	.40	.40	..	..
Jolly New Yorker, The. March and Two-Step	Weidt	B	.40	.15	.10	.20
Jolly Sailors. March and Two-Step	Weidt	A	.40	.40	..	..
June Bride, The. Waltzes. (Allen)	Arr. Jacobs	C	.50	.25	.20	.35
Jungle Echoes. A Cocoanut Dance	Hildreth	B	.40	.15	.10	.20
Kalola. A Darktown Intermezzo	Weidt	A	.30	.30	.10	.20
Katie. Waltz. (Potter)	Arr. Jacobs	A	.40	.15	.10	.20
Kentucky Wedding Knot. Novelty Two-Step	Arr. Jacobs	B	.40	.15	.10	.20
Kidder, The. Characteristic March. (Bushnell)	Arr. Jacobs	B	.40	.15	.10	.20
Kiss of Spring. (Rolfe)	Arr. Jacobs	A	.40	.25	.20	.35
Koonville Koonlets. Characteristic Cake Walk	Weidt	B	.40	.40	.10	.20
La Ballerina. Caprice	Lansing	B	.30	..	..	..
Lady Rose. Waltz. (Stevens)	Arr. Jacobs-Hildreth	B	.40	.15	.10	.20
Laughing Sam. Characteristic March. (Rolfe)	Arr. Jacobs	A	.40	.15	.10	.20
La Vota Schottische	De Lano	A	.40	.40	.10	.20
Lazy Luke. A Raggy Drag. (Philpot)	Arr. Hildreth-Jacobs	B	.40	.15	.10	.20
Light Heart. Polka	Weidt	A	.30	.30	.10	.20
Lilies of the Valley. Waltz	Weidt	A	.30	.30	.10	.20
Little Aristocrat. Petite Danse	Weidt	B	.40	.15	.10	.20
Little Duchess. Waltz	Kenneth	A	.40	.40	.10	.20
Little Sparkers. Danse Brillante	Lansing	A	.40	.15	.10	.20
Little Sunbeam Waltz	De Lano	A	.40	.40	.10	.20
Live Wire. March	Bone	B	.40	..	..	..
Loella Waltz	Weidt	C	.50	.25	.20	.35
Manana. Chilian Dance. (Missud)	Arr. Jacobs	B	.40	.15	.10	.20
Marconigram, The. March and Two-Step (Allen)	Arr. Jacobs	B	.40	.15	.10	.20
Masterstroke, The. Military March. (Lampe)	Arr. Hildreth	B	.40	.15	.10	.20
May Belle. Schottische	Weidt	A	.30	.30	.10	.20
Men of Harvard. March and Two-Step	Arr. Hildreth-Jacobs	B	.40	.15	.10	.20
Merry Monarch, The. March and Two-Step	Arr. Jacobs	B	.40	.15	.10	.20
Military Hero, The. March and Two-Step	Kenneth	A	.40	.15	.10	.20
Minor Jig	Kenneth	A	.30	..	..	..
Minstrel Echoes	Kenneth	B	.60	.60	.20	..
Montclair Galop	Weidt	A	.40	.40	.10	.20
My Dusky Rose. Schottische. (Allen)	Arr. Jacobs-Hildreth	B	.40	.15	.10	.20
My Old Kentucky Home. With Variations	Arr. Lansing	B	.40	..	..	.20
My Old Kentucky Home and Fair Harvard	Arr. Jacobs	A	.30	.15	.10	.20
Myra Waltz	Bemis	A	.40	.40	.10	.20
Myriad Dancer, The. Valse Ballet. (Allen)	Arr. Jacobs	B	.40	.15	.10	.20
New Arrival, The. March and Two-Step	Brazil	A	.40	.15	.10	.20
Northern Lights. Overture	Weidt	C	.50	.25	.20	.35
Old Acquaintance. March	Kenneth	B	.40	.40	..	..
Ole Black Mammy. Coon Shuffle	Lansing	B	.40	..	..	..
Ole Sambo. A Coon Serenade	Weidt	A	.40	.40	.10	.20
Onion Rag. A Bermuda Essence	Weidt	A	.40	.15	.10	.20
On Venice Waters	Reeder-Derwin	C	.30	..	..	..
On Boston Common. March and Two-Step	Bemis	B	.40	.15	.10	.20
Oshkosh Chief, The. March and Two-Step	Arr. Jacobs	B	.40	.15	.10	.20
Our Director. March. (Bigelow)	Arr. Lansing	A	.40	.15	.10	.20
Over the Waves. Waltzes. (Rosas)	Arr. Jacobs	B	.50	.50	.20	.35
Pavana. Entr'Acte. (Allen)	Arr. Jacobs	B	.40	.15	.10	.20
Pepeeta. Vals Espanol	Hildreth	B	.40	.15	.10	.20
Persian Lamb Rag. A Pepperette. (Wenrich)	Arr. Jacobs	B	.40	.15	.10	.20
Pickaninny Pranks. Cake Walk Characteristique	Jacobs	B	.40	.15	.10	.20
Pixies, The. Dance Characteristic. (Farrand)	Arr. Jacobs	A	.40	.15	.10	.20
Pizzicati. From "Sylvia." (Delibes)	Arr. Grout	B	.30	..	..	.20
Pokey Pete. Characteristic March. (Lerman)	Arr. Jacobs	B	.40	.15	.10	.20
Pretty Mamie Clancy. Medley Waltz	Arr. Hildreth	B	.40	.15	.10	.20
Pride of the Prairie. March and Two-Step	Arr. Hildreth	B	.40	.15	.10	.20
Prince Charming. Waltz. (Duffell)	Arr. Jacobs	A	.40	.40	.10	.20
Prince of India, The. March. (Farrand)	Arr. Jacobs	B	.40	.25	.20	.35
Queen of Roses. Waltzes	Weidt	C	.50	.25	.20	.35
Rag Tag. March and Two-Step	Weidt	A	.40	.15	.10	.20
Raiders, The. Galop	Weidt	A	.30	.30	.10	.20
Red Rover, The. March	Weidt	A	.30	.30	.10	.20
Rollicking Rube. Breakdown	Kenneth	A	.40	.40	.10	.20
Runabout, The. March and Two-Step	Arr. Hildreth-Jacobs	A	.40	.15	.10	.20
Sand Dance. Moonlight on the Suwanee	Arr. Lansing	B	.40	.15	.10	.20
Scissors to Grind. March and Two-Step. (Allen)	Arr. Jacobs	B	.40	.15	.10	.20
Sissy Giggles. Characteristic March	Arr. Hildreth-Jacobs	B	.40	.15	.10	.20
Sky High. Galop	Gibbons	A	.40	..	..	..
Smiling Sally. Caprice	Lansing	A	.30	.30	.10	.20
Soap Bubbles. Characteristic March	Arr. Jacobs-Hildreth	B	.40	.15	.10	.20
Social Lion, The. March and Two-Step	Hildreth	B	.40	.15	.10	.20
Song and Dance Schottische	Kenneth	A	.40	.40	.10	.20
Soralia. Spanish March. (Borel-Clerc)	Arr. Jacobs-Hildreth	B	.40	.15	.10	.20
Southern Pastimes. Schottische. (Wheeler)	Arr. Jacobs	A	.40	.15	.10	.20
Spanish Dance. No. 1. (Moszkowski)	Arr. Jacobs	C	.40	.40	.10	.20
Speedway, The. Galop	Weidt	A	.40	.15	.10	.20
Sporty Maid, The. March and Two-Step.	Arr. Jacobs-Hildreth	A	.40	.15	.10	.20
Story-Teller Waltzes, The. (Farrand)	Arr. Jacobs	B	.50	.25	.20	.35
Summer Breezes. Waltz	Lansing	A	.30	.30	.10	.20
Summer Girl, The. Waltz	Weidt	A	.30	.30	.10	.20
Summer Secrets. Waltz. (Taubert)	Arr. Jacobs-Hildreth	B	.50	.25	.20	.35
Sweet and Low and Forsaken	Arr. Lansing	C	.30	..	..	..
Sweet Corn. Characteristic March	Weidt	B	.40	.15	.10	.20
Tehama. Intermezzo Romantique. (Haines)	Arr. Jacobs	B	.40	.15	.10	.20
Tiptopper, A. March and Two-Step. (Corey)	Arr. Jacobs	B	.40	.15	.10	.20
Topsy's Recreation. A Dance (with Guitar Acc.)	Kenneth	B	.40	..	.40	..
True Blue. March and Two-Step	Kenneth	A	.40	.15	.10	.20
Under Palm and Pine. March and Two-Step	Kenneth	B	.40	.15	.10	.20
Under the Double Eagle. March. (Wagner)	Arr. Jacobs	B	.40	.40	.10	.20
Veritas. March and Two-Step. (Densmore)	Arr. Lansing	B	.40	.15	.10	.20
Victorious Harvard. March and Two-Step	Arr. Hildreth	B	.40	.15	.10	.20
Watch Hill. Two-Step	Kenneth	A	.40	.40	.10	.20
Whip and Spur. Galop. (Allen)	Arr. Jacobs	B	.40	.15	.10	.20
White Crow, The. March Oddity	Eno	B	.40	.15	.10	.20
"Who Dar!" Cake Walk and Two-Step. (Soule)	Arr. Jacobs	A	.40	.15	.10	.20
Wild Flowers. Schottische	Weidt	A	.40	.15	.10	.20
Yankee Boys. March	Weidt	A	.30	.30	.10	.20
Yankee Dandy. Characteristic March	Weidt	A	.40	.15	.10	.20
Yazoo Buck. Wing Dance. (Godfrey)	Arr. Jacobs	A	.40	.15	.10	.20
Zeona. Waltzes. (Arnold)	Arr. Jacobs	B	.50	.25	.20	.35
Zophiel. Intermezzo. (Hildreth)	Arr. Jacobs	B	.40	.15	.10	.20
Zulu Moon Dance. A Midnight Diversion	Odell	B	.40	.15	.10	.20

WALTER JACOBS, 167 Tremont St., Boston, Mass.

FOR ALL No 1 INSTRVMENTS

JACOBS' GRAND ORCHESTRA FOLIO

FOURTEEN POPULAR STANDARD — **COMPOSITIONS BY FAMOUS WRITERS**

INSTRUMENTATION AND PRICES

PLAYABLE IN ANY COMBINATION

1st Violin	.25	Flute	.25	Trombone	.25	1st Mandolin	.25
2d Violin	.25	1st Clarinet	.25	Drums	.25	2d Mandolin	.25
Viola	.25	2d Clarinet	.25	Horns	.25	3d Mandolin and Octave Mandola	.25
'Cello	.25	1st Cornet	.25	Oboe	.25	Guitar Acc.	.25
Bass	.25	2d Cornet	.25	Bassoon	.25	Banjo Acc.	.25

BANJO SOLO .50 **GUITAR SOLO** .50 **PIANO ACC.** .50

NOTE—There is a separate book, containing the entire fourteen numbers, for each of the twenty-three instruments listed above

CONTENTS

WALTER JACOBS, 167 TREMONT ST. BOSTON MASS